HEY GANG! WE'RE GONNA BE ON TV!

It's true! Bear Country School has its own TV station! Brother Bear, Bonnie, Queenie, and Too-Tall and the gang are not only running it, they're STARS! First graders are asking for their autographs.

But when the time comes for the station biggies to get their *parents'* autographs on failed test papers, the brilliant TV picture begins to roll, fade, and break up.

Will the school TV station be a hit—or a

DISASTER?

BIG CHAPTER BOOKS

The Berenstain Bears' MEDIA MADNESS

by the Berenstains

A BIG CHAPTER BOOK™

Random House New York

Library of Congress Cataloging-in-Publication Data
Berenstain, Stan.
The Berenstain bears' media madness /
by Stan and Jan Berenstain.
  p. cm. — (A big chapter book)
SUMMARY: When Bear Country School is allowed to run a television station, the cubs become very involved and neglect their studies.
ISBN 0-679-86664-7 (pbk.) — ISBN 0-679-96664-1 (lib. bdg.)
[1. Television broadcasting—Fiction.
2. Television stations—Fiction. 3. Schools—Fiction
4. Bears—Fiction.] I. Berenstain, Jan. II. Title.
III. Series: Berenstain, Stan. Big chapter book.
PZ7.B4483Beah   1995
[Fic]—dc20   94-40741

Manufactured in the United States of America 10 9 8 7 6 5 4 3 2 1

BIG CHAPTER BOOKS is a trademark of Berenstain Enterprises, Inc.

Contents

Chapter 1
The Calm Before the Storm

Everything was going pretty smoothly at Bear Country School—a little too smoothly. The students were studying. The teachers were teaching. Mr. Honeycomb, the principal, was running the school the way he always had.

The sports teams were winning and losing about the same number of games they had the year before. Miss Glitch was still giving cubs bad grades for saying "who" when they should have said "whom." Mr. Grizzmeyer was still giving out extra laps and push-ups to cubs who messed up in gym.

Brother Bear and Bonnie Brown were still sort of paired off. Ferdy Factual and Trudy Brunowitz were still good nerd buddies. Too-Tall Grizzly and Queenie McBear's on-again off-again "thing" was on again and off again. Brother, Sister, Cousin Fred, and Lizzy Bruin still walked to and from school together.

The fact that they were always together annoyed Too-Tall for some reason.

"Well, if it isn't the Boresome Foursome," said Too-Tall when they arrived at school.

But Brother wasn't in the mood to take any guff from Too-Tall and his gang of schoolyard bullies. "Why don't you shut up, Too-Tall?" he said. "The fact that we come to school together is no skin off your nose."

"Oh, yeah?" snarled Too-Tall. "Wanna make somethin' out of it?" He bunched up his big fists.

"Looks to me like Mother Nature already has," said Brother. "A bowling ball!"

"Hey, that's a pretty good one, chief," said gang member Skuzz.

Too-Tall did have a pretty big nose. For a second, it looked as if a big fight might break out right then and there.

But Too-Tall just sighed and relaxed his fists. "Forget it," he said. "Punching you out just isn't worth breaking the boredom."

Brother and Too-Tall had tangled before. Brother was the only cub willing to stand up to Too-Tall.

"Hey," said Queenie McBear. "Why don't you two kiss and make up?"

"No thanks," said Too-Tall. "But I wouldn't mind kissing *you* a little." He puckered his mouth and made wet kissing noises.

"Down, boy," said Queenie. "I don't think I could take the excitement."

Cousin Fred sighed. Babs Bruno sighed.

The little run-in between Brother and Too-Tall was the closest thing to excitement that had happened at Bear Country School in days.

Brother Bear sighed. Too-Tall sighed. Skuzz, Smirk, and Vinnie sighed. If a sky-writing plane had flown overhead at that moment and spelled out BORING, nobody would have been surprised.

"Has anybody seen Bonnie?" said Brother.

There were shrugs and head shakes all around.

What Brother and his friends didn't know was that Bonnie had come to school early that morning. She had come with her uncle,

Squire Grizzly, in his chauffeur-driven limousine. At that very moment, she and the squire were in Mr. Honeycomb's office, talking to the principal about something special that was going to happen—something that would cut through the boredom like a hot knife through butter!

It was something that would take Bear Country School by storm, something that would take hold of its students and teachers like a powerful virus. It would bring the law down on Mr. Honeycomb and almost get Teacher Bob *fired*.

That something was...*media madness!*

Chapter 2
The Gift Horse

"What do you think?" asked Brother at lunch later that day. "Should the school accept Squire Grizzly's gift? That equipment is pretty old, you know."

"Of course we should," said Cousin Fred. "You know what they say—never look a gift horse in the mouth."

"What the heck do horses have to do with it?" said Barry Bruin.

"It's just an expression," said Babs Bruno. "It means that if someone gives you a horse, you shouldn't worry too much about whether it has good teeth or not."

"Horses? Teeth?" said Barry. "We're talking about a television station. A whole television station that Squire Grizzly wants to
give to Bear Country School. That's news!
Big news!"

Barry was right, of course. This was big
news. That evening the newspaper even had
a story about it on the front page.

"Look at this," said Papa Bear. He read
the headline out loud. " 'Philanthropist
Squire Grizzly Gives TV Station to Bear
Country School.' "

Sister Bear came over to Papa's easy chair

and looked down at the headline. "What's a *phil-an-thro-pist?*" she asked.

"Well," said Papa. "Er...it's a rich guy who...er...likes to give stuff away."

Sister looked at Mama with a question in her eyes.

"That's close enough, dear," said Mama.

" 'Squire Grizzly,' " read Papa, " 'who owns the Grizzly Gas Station chain, Grizzly Supermarkets, and Great Grizzly National Bank, is said to be the richest bear in Bear Country. But it is his television interests that led to his unusual gift to Bear Country School.' " Papa began reading the story to himself.

"Well, let's hear the rest of the story," said Mama.

"Huh? Oh," said Papa. "Well, the squire owns station WBBC in Big Bear City. According to the story, he's putting new state-of-the-art equipment into the station, and he's giving all his old equipment to Bear Country School. Hey, this part is interesting. It says, 'It is reported that the idea for the gift came from the squire's niece, Miss Bonnie Brown, a student at Bear Country School.' Isn't that *your* Bonnie Brown, Brother?"

"Well, we *are* friends," said Brother, blushing.

"Did you and Sister know about this gift to the school?" asked Mama.

"Oh, sure," said Sister.

"It was announced at morning assembly," said Brother.

"Why didn't you mention it?" asked Papa.

"Mostly because Mr. Honeycomb hasn't decided whether to accept it yet," said Brother. "They're having a big meeting tomorrow to decide."

"Why wouldn't they accept it?" asked Mama.

"Some of the teachers don't like television," said Brother. "Miss Glitch, for instance. She says television is 'destroying the minds of our country's youth.' "

"She said that?" said Papa.

"Many times," said Sister. "And when Mr. Honeycomb was talking about it at assembly, Mr. Grizzmeyer made a face."

Chapter 3
Let's Party!

Brother, Sister, Cousin Fred, and the rest of their group were gathered around Too-Tall in the schoolyard.

"That's right," Too-Tall was saying. "It's a done deal. Mr. Honeycomb accepted the TV equipment on behalf of Bear Country School."

Bonnie was surprised. "How do you know that?" she asked. "My uncle hasn't even been told yet."

"I got ways, sweet cakes," said Too-Tall, making goo-goo eyes at Bonnie.

Queenie put her arm in Too-Tall's. "It's very simple," she said proudly. "He's got a special listening spot in the broom closet next to the faculty meeting room."

"How'd the meeting go?" asked Cousin Fred.

"Well," said Too-Tall. "Glitch and Grizzmeyer voted 'Against.' Teacher Bob and Teacher Jane voted 'For.' Mr. Honeycomb voted 'For' and broke the tie. You know what that means, kiddos? It means we're all gonna be on TV! We're all gonna be stars! So...*Let's party!*"

Too-Tall grabbed Queenie, and the two of them started dancing. The other cubs made

a circle around them and began clapping.
But Brother didn't join the happy circle. He
was standing off to one side, looking serious.

"Why so serious?" asked Bonnie. "Aren't
you excited about the new TV station?"

"I guess so," said Brother. "But I have a

funny feeling about it. You know—sort of like before a storm, when the air smells funny and it feels like all heck is about to break loose."

"Look!" said Bonnie.

A truck that said WBBC on the side and had a satellite dish on top was pulling in. It backed up to the school's loading platform.

"That's one of my uncle's remote trucks," said Bonnie. "Come on. Let's watch."

Brother, Bonnie, and a bunch of other cubs ran to the loading platform. They watched as the driver and his helper unloaded all kinds of TV equipment. There were cameras, reflectors, boxes of sound equipment, and what seemed like miles of thick black cable. The driver and helper piled everything on the loading platform and started to leave.

"Hey!" called Mr. Honeycomb. "You can't

just leave this stuff out here on the platform!"

A radio was squawking in the remote
truck.

"Got no choice, sir!" shouted the driver.
"We have to go do a remote on a train
wreck just outside Big Bear City!"

Off they zoomed.

"Oh, dear!" said Mr. Honeycomb. "What
is all this equipment? It looks valuable." He
looked up at the cloudy sky. "What if it
rains?"

"It's valuable all right," said Teacher Bob.

"*Very* valuable."

"Huh? Oh, it's you, Bob."

"It may be 'used,'" said Teacher Bob, "but it's first-class equipment. And you're right, Mr. Honeycomb. Rain would ruin it. Hey, Too-Tall! Come over here and bring your gang! We need some muscle!"

"Coming, teach!" said Too-Tall. "Hey, you gonna put us on TV? Me and the gang are rap artists."

"Maybe later," said Teacher Bob. "For now I just want you and your associates to carry this stuff into school and place it

carefully in the storeroom behind the auditorium. You can help, too, Brother. And Bonnie, you can supervise."

"Look out for the snake, Bonnie!" shouted Too-Tall. He switched one of the big black cables back and forth.

Bonnie just laughed and jumped aside. "Too-Tall," she said, "I've spent more time around TV cable than you've spent on suspension. Hey, careful with that camera. Don't try to carry it by yourself. It needs two of you. That's better. And for Pete's sake, don't drag the cable. Wrap it around the stand."

Chapter 4
A Word to the Wise

"You seem to be familiar with this equipment, Bob," said Mr. Honeycomb as the cubs carried it into the school.

"A little," said Teacher Bob. "I used to help out sometimes at the university TV station. But mostly I worked at the radio station. That's how I worked my way through college. I announced, read the news, discjockeyed, ran the engineering. And I was

station manager during my senior year."

"I'll come right to the point, Bob," said the principal. "How would you like to manage our TV station?"

"I'd sure like to give it a shot," said Teacher Bob.

"Then it's settled. You'll have some help getting started. The squire is sending over one of his experts to help set things up. Miss Glitch and Mr. Grizzmeyer are going to be pretty upset. But don't worry. I'll handle them."

"Upset?" said Teacher Bob.

"I was surprised when they both wanted

to manage the station," said Mr. Honey-comb.

"But they were *against* the station," said Teacher Bob. "Miss Glitch hates television. And Mr. Grizzmeyer...well, you know Mr. Grizzmeyer." Teacher Bob grinned.

"I do, indeed," said the principal. "I guess they thought 'If you can't beat 'em, join 'em.' Miss Glitch wants to do a program on language arts. You know—grammar, punctuation, parts of speech. And you can guess what Mr. Grizzmeyer has in mind."

"Yep," said Teacher Bob. "I can just hear him: 'The three most important words in physical education are *calisthenics, calisthenics*, and *calisthenics*.' "

"Well, I'll deal with them," said Mr. Honeycomb. "A word to the wise, though. You might want to let them have some input on the programming."

"Sure thing," said Teacher Bob.

Brother and Bonnie hadn't exactly been snooping. But they couldn't help hearing what was said. When the bell rang to end recess, they got in line and filled their friends in on the news—that Teacher Bob was going to run the new school station.

"Another word to the wise," said the principal as he and Teacher Bob headed back into the building. "Don't get carried away with this TV thing. Remember, it's an extra. Be sure to keep your class up to speed in their regular schoolwork: English, math, science, social studies, geography—the works."

"Absolutely," said Teacher Bob. "You can count on it."

But words of warning, even to the wise, don't always work. Especially when it comes to something as exciting as television.

Chapter 5
We're All Gonna Be on TV!

The cubs beat Teacher Bob back to class. When he got there, they were buzzing with excitement.

"Hey, teach," said Too-Tall. "Are you gonna make us all TV stars?"

"You oughta put me in charge, teacher," said Barry Bruin.

"Why you, birdbrain?" said Queenie McBear.

"Because I know TV backwards and forwards," said Barry. "I watch more TV than all the rest of you put together."

"Sure," said Babs Bruno. "That's why you're so dumb. It's like Miss Glitch says. TV has destroyed your mind."

"Oh, yeah?" said Barry. "Get a load of my stand-up." He stood up on his chair and raised his arms like a TV comic. "Welcome to *The Barry Bruin Comedy Hour!* I just flew in from Big Bear City...and *boy, are my arms tired!* Take my mom...*please!* A horse walks into a bar and the bartender says, 'Why the long face?' "

By now the cubs were groaning and holding their noses.

"Sit down!" shouted Queenie.

"I can do sit-down, too," said Barry. He sat down. "My motel room is so small that we have to sleep three in a bed—me, the doorknob, and the sink. Or how about this one..."

Too-Tall loomed over Barry. "Queenie meant sit down and *shut up!*"

"All right now, settle down," said Teacher Bob. "Back in your seat, please, Too-Tall."

"But, teach," said Too-Tall. "Me and the gang would be cool on TV."

"What are you going to do for an act?" said Babs Bruno. "Punch cubs out?"

"Perish the thought, sweetheart," said Too-Tall. "We're *rap artists*."

"What, may I ask, is a 'rap artist'?" said class genius Ferdy Factual, who didn't keep up with musical trends.

"A rap artist, my fine feathered nerd," said Too-Tall, "is somebody who, if you don't shut up, will rap you in the mouth."

Trudy Brunowitz moved in between the two cubs. "Leave Ferdy alone, you big thug," she said to Too-Tall.

"Well, lah-dee-dah!" said Too-Tall, heading back to his seat. "The little nerd is gettin' protected by a *female* nerd!"

"That will be quite enough," said Teacher Bob. He was pretty easygoing, but he had

26

his tough side, too. And even Too-Tall knew when it was time to sit down and be quiet.

"Now," Teacher Bob went on, "the fact is, I have been placed in charge of the new school television station." The cubs clapped loudly. "Settle down, please. This is going to be *your* station. So I do want to hear your ideas. But only if you raise your hand and speak when called on. Yes, Babs."

"I think art and culture are very important," said Babs. "We should have some kind of cultural show. You know—

poetry, book reviews, music reviews."

"Thank you, Babs," said Teacher Bob. "Ferdy?"

It was no surprise that Ferdy suggested a science show. Queenie wanted a special news show—one that would uncover Bear Country's dark secrets. Barry, of course, begged for a comedy show.

Just about every kind of show ever heard of was suggested. As the discussion went on, cubs forgot about raising their hands and waiting to be called on. They started

jumping up and shouting. But Teacher Bob didn't really mind. It had been a pretty dull school year, and it was good to see the cubs excited about something again.

But there was someone out in the hall listening—someone who was *not* so easygoing. Miss Glitch. And she looked angry.

"Humph!" she said, just as Mr. Grizzmeyer happened to pass by.

"A problem, Miss Glitch?" asked Mr. Grizzmeyer.

"I don't know how I'm supposed to grade papers with all that racket going on," she said.

Just then Teacher Bob saw Miss Glitch out of the corner of his eye. He smiled at her and gently closed his classroom door to keep the noise in.

"Principal's pet—that's what he is!" said Miss Glitch. "I was talking to my friend at the Board of Education. Mr. Television won't be so high-and-mighty when..." She stopped short, as if she had said more than she'd planned.

"When what?" asked Mr. Grizzmeyer.

"Never you mind," said Miss Glitch. She turned and went back into her classroom.

Mr. Grizzmeyer was left standing in the hall wondering what *that* was all about.

Chapter 6
Keep It Simple, Stupid

Meanwhile, back in Teacher Bob's room, the class had just about run out of ideas and suggestions.

Teacher Bob turned to Brother Bear. "What about you, Brother?" he said. "You haven't come up with any ideas. Aren't you excited about the school television station?"

"I guess so," said Brother. "But I've been thinking..."

"I thought I smelled wood burning," said Too-Tall. But nobody laughed, not even Too-Tall's gang. They were all wrapped up in the discussion.

"It seems to me," said Brother, "that this television thing is going to take some real planning. It's not going to be like organizing a stickball game. There are all kinds of questions. Like who's going to be in charge? And who's going to do what?"

Brother didn't notice that Teacher Bob was writing the words "planning" and "organization" on the board.

"And what kind of shows are we going to put on?" Brother continued. "We don't want to embarrass ourselves by putting on junk. What makes a good show? First, it's gotta be fun to watch…"

Teacher Bob wrote "entertainment value" on the board.

"And since this is going to be a *school* station," Brother said, "it should have some educational programs."

Teacher Bob added "educational value" to the list on the board.

"But it's not going to matter what kind of shows we put on if we mess up," said Brother. "You know—run around like chickens with our heads cut off, knocking over cameras and forgetting our words."

"Yeah," said Cousin Fred. "Like when Barry forgot his words in the school play and just stared out at the audience like a goofball."

Teacher Bob smiled and added "production values" to his list. He underlined it three times and put three exclamation points after it.

Meanwhile, someone had started clapping, slowly and loudly. It was Bonnie Brown. She had stood up and was looking at Brother. "Brother, I could kiss you," she said.

"How about me?" said Too-Tall and most of the other boys, sticking out their cheeks or puckering their lips.

Brother just blushed.

"Do you have something to tell us, Bonnie?" said Teacher Bob. He certainly hoped so. Bonnie knew more about television than everyone else in the room put together. She was a professional. And it was Bonnie who had given Squire Grizzly the idea to donate the station to Bear Country School in the first place.

"I've been holding back because I don't want to come across as a show-off," she said. "But as most of you know, I've done a lot of television work. I've modeled and acted in commercials. I've even done small parts on soap operas. And I have to tell you: My friend Brother Bear just said a mouthful."

Brother had gotten over his blush and was now grinning like a smile button.

"Running a television station *is* exciting," Bonnie continued. "But you always have to remember that it's about basics. All those things Brother said and Teacher Bob wrote on the board are true. Television has to be entertaining. It should have some educational value, too, especially if it's school television. But most of all, it's got to have what Teacher Bob calls 'production values.' Which brings me back to the word KISS. It's a big idea in the television business. But it has nothing to do with kissing. It's an *acronym*. Cousin Fred, do your thing."

"Sure," said Fred, who read the dictionary for fun. "Ac-ro-nym. A form in which the initial letters of the words in a slogan or phrase are treated as a word."

"Thank you, Fred," said Bonnie. "KISS stands for *keep it simple, stupid*. And that's exactly what we have to do if this television station is going to make it: remember to *keep it simple, stupid*."

KEEP IT SIMPLE, STUPID.

Brother and Bonnie had given the class a
lot to think about. As everyone sat and
thought, Bertha Broom raised her hand.
Though Bertha was a girl, she was so big
and strong that she played on many of the
school sports teams with the boys. And she
was also a brown belt in karate. Usually she
didn't have much to say. But when she
spoke, cubs listened.

"Yes, Bertha," said Teacher Bob.

Bertha stood up. "I think what Brother
and Bonnie said makes a lot of sense. So I

say...*let's hear it for Brother and Bonnie!*"

Bertha started to clap. Her big hands coming together sounded like pistol shots. The other cubs took the hint and joined in the applause. Only Skuzz, Smirk, and Vinnie didn't join in. Until, that is, Too-Tall snarled, "You heard Bertha, you creeps! Let's hear it for Brother and Bonnie!"

Then Teacher Bob took the hint, too. "I move that Bonnie Brown be program director of our new station and that Brother Bear be general manager," he said. "Those opposed?"

Silence.

"Those in favor?"

A roar of *yays*.

There was a lot of back-patting and high-fiving as the class congratulated Brother and Bonnie. In fact, there was so much noise that nobody noticed when the bell rang for the end of the school day.

"Class dismissed!" shouted Teacher Bob.

There was something else that no one noticed. The class had not done a single bit of regular schoolwork since morning recess. And for the first time for as long as anyone could remember, Teacher Bob hadn't given out *any homework!*

Chapter 7
Things to Do

While Teacher Bob didn't give his class any homework for that night, he gave himself quite a lot. After he and his wife put their two preschoolers to bed, he placed a sheet of paper in his typewriter and typed steadily until he had made the following list.

THINGS TO DO

1. Call WBBC expert and arrange visit to school.
2. Study instruction books that came with equipment (in plastic bag tied to one of the cameras).
3. Inspect all equipment.
4. Assign class members to station jobs (bring in cubs from other classes later).
5. Check with school custodian, Grizzly Gus, about school's electrical setup. Can it handle station's needs?
6. Decide on station call letters.
7. Work out broadcast schedule: how many days a week, how long each day.
8. Post notice on main bulletin board asking students for program ideas.
9. Check working order of all classroom TV sets.
10. Pray!

After finishing his list, Teacher Bob rolled another sheet into place and typed the following:

IMPORTANT ANNOUNCEMENT

PROGRAM IDEAS WANTED

Be the first cub in your class to have a program on the exciting new Bear Country School television station. All submissions must include your name, your teacher's name, and a description of your program idea in 200 words or less. Submit all ideas to Bonnie Brown, Program Director.

Teacher Bob didn't get to bed until quite late. That was a worry, because he knew the next day would be a busy one and he wanted to get to school extra early. As if that weren't bad enough, the events of the day and all the things turning over in his mind made it hard for him to fall asleep.

When Teacher Bob finally did fall asleep, he had the weirdest dream. It was about Miss Glitch. And in the dream, she was a *witch*.

TV TABLE OF ORGANIZATION
PROGRAM DIRECTOR - BONNIE BROWN
GENERAL MANAGER - BROTHER BEAR
TECHNICAL DIRECTOR - FERDY FACTUAL
WRITER - TRUDY BRUNOWITZ
RESEARCH - COUSIN FRED
LIGHTING - BABS BRUNO
- BERTHA BROOM
- BARRY BRUIN
F OF SECURITY - TOO-TALL GRIZZLY
TIES - VINNIE, SKUZZ, SMIRK

Chapter 8
Clear for Action!

Teacher Bob usually started class in a relaxed, easygoing way. But today he was all business.

"In your seats, everyone," he said. "We've got a lot to do. If you look at the front blackboard, you'll see that I've written down all your lessons for the day."

"Boy," Cousin Fred whispered to Brother, "he must have come in early to put all that on the board."

"I'll have to be out of the room a lot working on the television project," said Teacher Bob. "Bertha will be in charge while I'm gone. On the side board, you see what I call our 'TV Table of Organization.' It shows which TV jobs I've given to which cubs."

Too-Tall was listed as "Chief of Security," with Skuzz, Smirk, and Vinnie listed as deputies.

"Hey, get this, everybody," said Too-Tall, puffing his chest out with pride. "Anybody who so much as lays a hand on one of those cameras goes down for the count!"

"Please take charge now, Bertha," said

Teacher Bob. "I'm going to meet with the expert from WBBC. Brother, Bonnie, Ferdy, and Trudy, please come with me." He was sure Bertha could handle the job. Too-Tall and the gang were much more scared of Bertha than they were of any teacher.

The expert from WBBC was already inspecting the equipment and checking the electrical outlets. He wasted no time in telling Teacher Bob about some of the problems they were going to have to deal with. The trouble was that the expert spoke a language that Teacher Bob didn't understand.

"Yer frammis grammis isn't gonna fit yer ruckus gruckus," he said. "And furthermore, yer rollagonk is outa whack with yer zantac."

Luckily, Ferdy and Trudy seemed to

YER ROLLAGONK
IS OUTA WHACK WITH
YER ZANTAC...

understand him perfectly.

"I take your point, sir," said Ferdy. "But I would suggest that you bypass the frammis grammis and plug it directly into the zantac."

"Good thinking, son," said the expert.

"I think we'd better let Ferdy and Trudy deal with Mr. Frammis Grammis," Teacher Bob told Brother and Bonnie. "We've got a lot of decisions to make."

They met in a corner of the room to talk

things over. They decided that the new school station would telecast for a half-hour a day during the last school period, five days a week. They also decided to rehearse in the morning before school started and broadcast live in the afternoon. They would need to have their decisions okayed by Mr. Honeycomb. Teacher Bob said he would take care of that.

Meanwhile, Ferdy, Trudy, and the expert got the equipment working. Soon they had a test pattern on a monitor. But it said WBBC!

"We're going to need our own call letters," said Teacher Bob as they headed back to class.

He wasn't pleased when they got there. "What's going on?" he said. "This doesn't look like schoolwork."

The cubs were calling out funny-sound-ing words, and Bertha was writing them on the board.

"We were working on the lessons," said Bertha Broom, "but somebody brought up the idea of call letters for our new station."

"Somehow, WOOP and KLUG don't do it for me," said Bonnie. She went to the board, picked up the chalk, and wrote "BTV." "It stands for *Bear-TV*," she said. "What do you think, gang?"

"I vote yes!" said Bertha.

"Me too," said Too-Tall.

The other cubs all nodded.

"Well, I guess that decides it," said Teacher Bob. "BTV it is."

Chapter 9
Putting It Together

The open talent auditions took place in the school auditorium. They lasted a long time. It seemed as if every cub in Bear Country School wanted to star on television.

But it wasn't too hard to decide who could sing and who couldn't, who could dance and who was a klutz, or who had a good speaking voice and who sounded like a frog. BTV's management group sat in the audience and took notes while the "wannabe" anchorbears, singer bears, and stand-up bears did their thing.

"Thank you, we'll get back to you," said Bonnie after each performance.

Too-Tall's security team kept order without getting too physical. Teacher Bob did say no to one of Too-Tall's ideas, though. The gang leader had made a long-handled hook from a window pole and a bent coat hanger.

"It works like this, teach," said Too-Tall. "If some singer hits a sour note or some dancer trips over his own feet, I just give 'em the hook. I reach out and drag 'em off

the stage. It's a great gimmick. It saves time, and it's a million laughs. I know. I seen it on the network."

"*Saw,* Too-Tall," said Teacher Bob.

"Same difference, teach. If somebody hits a sour note on a musical saw, I just reach out and…"

"No hook," said Teacher Bob. "Do you hear me?"

"Loud and clear, teach," said Too-Tall in a hurt tone of voice.

There was a big response to the request for program ideas. Tons of ideas came flooding in. Sorting them out wasn't easy. It became clear that a system was needed.

"How's this sound?" said Brother. "We'll have an A pile for the really good ones, a B pile for the okay ones…"

"And a PEE-YEW pile for the ones that stink!" said Queenie.

"How about this one?" said Barry Bruin. " 'My program is called *Ant Farm*. It will show the fascinating life of the mighty ant, which has been on the earth for millions of years.' "

"PEE-YEW!" said Queenie.

It took a lot of work, but five program ideas were finally chosen. The following notice was then sent to every classroom, with instructions that it be placed on the classroom bulletin board.

YOUR BTV PROGRAM GUIDE

Starting Monday, during club/study-hall period, BTV, your very own in-school television station, will begin its five-day-a-week schedule.

Monday: TALENT HUNT

An exciting program that will bring you talent from every class. There will be singers, dancers, jugglers, roller skaters—talents of every kind. A winning act will be selected each week by the student body. Later there will be an all-winners' show. The winner of that show will be awarded a chance at fame and fortune—an appearance on station WBBC in Big Bear City!

Tuesday: 30 MINUTES

Beware the cub with the minicam. He or she will be on the prowl for *your* story. So look out!

Wednesday: TOP THAT STUNT

A super-exciting show in which daredevil cubs try to TOP THAT STUNT.

Thursday: SUGGESTION BOX

An educational show about *your* school. Place your ideas for improving Bear Country School in the suggestion boxes in the school hallways.

Friday: BEAR COUNTRY GLADIATORS

A test of strength and courage in which cubs compete against Bertha Broom in various sports events and activities. The show will be hosted by Mr. Grizzmeyer.

Teacher Jane had message duty that day. When she delivered the pack of messages to Miss Glitch, the new BTV schedule was on top. Miss Glitch glanced at it.

"What do you think?" asked Teacher Jane.

Miss Glitch just smiled.

After Teacher Jane left, Miss Glitch looked at the schedule more carefully. Then, instead of putting it on the bulletin board, she crumpled it up and tossed it into the wastebasket.

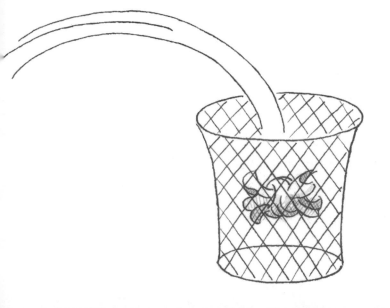

Chapter 10
Busy Weekend

It was Friday afternoon. The Boresome
Foursome, as Too-Tall called them, were
walking home from school.

"How come you didn't pick my program
idea?" said Sister.

"The board just didn't think watching a
bunch of cubs jumping rope would make a
good television show," said Brother. "And I
can't play favorites."

"Great," said Sister. "What's the good of
having a TV big shot for a brother if he
won't play favorites?"

As soon as Brother and Sister got home,

they went to the kitchen for their after-school milk and cookies.

"Please don't gobble your food," said Mama to Brother.

"That's how TV big shots eat," said Sister. "You ought to see him in the lunchroom with all the other TV big shots. They're out of the lunchroom in two minutes flat and back to their precious BTV."

"Excuse me, please," said Brother. "I'm going upstairs. I have a ton of homework to do."

"Mama?" said Sister after Brother had gone. "What's *comeuppance?*"

" 'Comeuppance?' " said Mama.

"Yeah. What's it mean?"

"Well," said Mama, "if someone did something you didn't like and then something bad happened to them, you might say they got their comeuppance. Why do you ask?"

"We had a special English lesson from Miss Glitch today. And some of the cubs started talking about the new television station. So Miss Glitch said, 'Never mind about that television station. They'll get their comeuppance.' "

"Hmm," said Mama. She was about to ask Sister a question or two. But Papa came in from his workshop and asked where Brother was.

"Upstairs doing homework," said Mama.

"Glad to hear it," said Papa.

Papa and Mama had been proud when Brother was made general manager of the school TV station. They thought it was good for him to get an early start on the "information superhighway" everyone was talking about. But they were worried about Brother keeping up with his regular schoolwork.

"What good is an early start on this 'information superhighway,'" said Papa, "if you can't do arithmetic or speak proper English, and don't know anything about science, history, and geography?"

So Papa and Mama felt good about Brother spending the weekend upstairs doing homework. But they might not have felt so good if they had known the *kind* of homework he was doing. All of it had to do with station BTV. There were scripts to edit, announcements to write, program ideas to comment on. Not one bit of it had to do with math, English, science, history, or geography.

Chapter 11
We're a Smash!

Brother, Bonnie, Cousin Fred, Queenie, and the other members of their group hoped BTV would be a success. And they worked hard to reach that goal. But none of them—certainly not Brother—expected it to be the huge success it turned out to be.

BTV was, quite simply, a smash. A *super* smash. A super-*duper* smash! It seemed that each day's show was a bigger hit than the one before. If ratings had been taken, BTV would have had the highest ratings in the history of television.

Not that everything went smoothly. Barry Bruin went blank when his cue card was held upside down. He stared at the audience like a goofball. Then Gil Grizzwold lost his shorts during *Top That Stunt.*

Some of the suggestions on *Suggestion Box* were pretty embarrassing, too. The worst was: "Why doesn't Mr. Honeycomb go on a diet? He's starting to look like the Goodbear blimp." The BTV group decided that they would have to screen the suggestions before air time.

But there was no question about it—BTV was a big success. Brother and Bonnie became such celebrities that it was almost embarrassing. A first grader even asked Brother for his autograph. And Teacher

Bob got calls from all over Bear Country. He was interviewed for the newspaper and invited to speak to the Businessbears' Club in Big Bear City.

There were surprises, too. Too-Tall and the gang did a rap number on the third *Talent Hunt*. Their song was a big hit. It won them the prize that week.

All make way!
This means you!
The Too-Tall gang
is comin' through!

We're the Too-Tall gang!
We stomp on toes;
We shake the ground
And stone the crows!

So look out, all
You dweebs and drips,
We're the four bad bears
of the Apocalypse.

All make way!
This means you!
The Too-Tall gang
is comin' through!

The gang had a little help with the words. They got the rhyme for "drips" from Cousin Fred. But everyone thought they were great. Even Bonnie. She thought they might even win the big prize!

Chapter 12
The Trouble with Success

Brother, Bonnie, and the whole BTV gang were in their favorite booth at the Burger Bear after a hard day at the station. They were discussing some problems over milk shakes. These were problems of success. But that didn't make them any easier to solve.

"That's the way it always is," said Queenie. "When you've got something good going, everybody wants to get into the act."

Queenie was right, of course. There was more talent than they could make room for on the hugely successful *Talent Hunt*. Good program ideas kept rolling in. But the schedule was already full.

"I don't know what the rest of you think," said Brother, "but I've been thinking that maybe, just *maybe*..."

"Maybe what?" said Bonnie.

"Maybe we should go for broke and stay on the air for an hour a day instead of a half-hour."

"Don't you mean *go* broke?" said Bonnie, shaking her head.

"How so?" said Brother.

"It would cost a fortune," said Bonnie. "Keeping the school open would cost a lot of money—for heat and light, for overtime pay for the school bus drivers. For all kinds of things."

"It would be great if we could do it," said Cousin Fred. "But Bonnie's right. And who knows if we'd even be *allowed* to keep the school open."

"May I have the floor?" said Ferdy Factual. He yawned one of those yawns that meant he was about to go into his genius act.

"Ferdy, you can have the whole building if you can figure out some way to lengthen our schedule without going broke," said Bonnie.

"All right," said Ferdy. "I've been thinking along the same lines as Brother. But, unlike him, I have anticipated the financial problems and solved them in advance. The solution is simple. It involves two basic ideas. First, we convert BTV from a closed-circuit in-school station to a low-power

MAY I HAVE THE FLOOR?

over-the-air station broadcasting to the community. Second, we sell commercials."

"Totally cool!" cried Queenie, almost spilling her shake. "Now you're talking my language! Ferdy, baby, you have just hit yourself a *humongous* tape-measure home run!"

"On the other hand," said Brother, "it may just be a long, loud foul. Don't you need some sort of license for an over-the-air television station? And what about power and a transmitter?"

"You may relax on those scores," said Ferdy. "It so happens that my esteemed uncle, Professor Actual Factual, has just such an over-the-air license. It's gathering dust in a drawer over at the Bearsonian Institution. It's made out to Professor Actual Factual and associates. I work for my uncle on Saturdays. Thus I am an associate.

I can also tell you that a low-power transmitter is child's play. All we have to do for power is hook up to the school emergency generator for an hour a day."

The cubs presented their plan to Teacher Bob. He presented it to Mr. Honeycomb. After a couple of deep breaths, Mr. Honeycomb said okay.

"Now hear this!" said Queenie. "If nobody objects, I'm placing myself in charge of selling commercials."

No one objected. Too-Tall came up with a slogan: "Buy time on BTV—*or else!*" But it was rejected.

Queenie chose Too-Tall, Babs Bruno, and Barry Bruin as her sales crew. Then she and her crew fanned out through Beartown with dollar signs in their eyes.

PAPA BEAR'S FINE FURNITURE
PAY TO: BTV ....
FIFTY ....
$50.00
DOLLARS

DR. GERT GRIZZLY $50.00
DOLLARS
PAY TO: BTV
Fifty 00/100 Grizzly

BEAR
Biff Bruin's Pharmacy $50.00
PAY TO: BTV .... 00/100 DOLLARS
FIFTY ———— BIFF BRUIN

$50.00
100 DOLLARS
Prof. A. Factual

Farmer Ben's Fancy Produce
PAY TO: BTV $50.00
FIFTY ————
00/100 DOLLARS
Farmer Ben

DR. BEARSON $5
PAY TO: BTV
FIFTY 00/100 Dr. B

Chapter 13
Commercials Galore

Queenie and company brought in tons of commercials.

"They never knew what hit them," she said. "We made 'em an offer they couldn't refuse. Every sponsor gets a thirty-second commercial and a terrific poster to put in their window. And they also get whatever production help they need to make the commercial."

"Holy cow!" said Brother when he saw

the pile of checks and contracts Queenie
had brought in. "Look, here's one from my
dad!" Printed on the check was "Papa Bear's
Fine Furniture."

"Here's one from Biff Bruin's Pharmacy,"
said Barry. "That's *my* dad!"

There were also checks from Dr. Gert
Grizzly, dentist Dr. Bearson, Farmer Ben's
Fancy Produce, and many others. There
would be more than enough money to make
the cubs' closed-circuit in-school station a
real over-the-air station. The station would
reach only two and a half miles in every
direction. But that covered most of
Beartown.

While Queenie sold commercials, Ferdy
and Trudy got Professor Actual Factual to
help them put together a small transmitter
and hook it up to the school's generator.
They set their signal for channel 17, an

empty channel in the Beartown area, and threw the switch. Right away calls came in telling them that BTV was being received all over Beartown.

Great excitement spread throughout Bear Country School. There was a big, proud smile on the face of just about everyone in the building. Even Miss Glitch was smiling.

But Miss Glitch's smile wasn't a smile of pride. It was the smile of someone who knew something that nobody else knew.

MONDAY

TUESDAY

WEDNESDAY

THURSDAY

FRIDAY

Chapter 14
Going Public

Brother, Bonnie, and the whole BTV crew worked harder than ever to get the new schedule ready for broadcasting. When it was finally ready, this is what it looked like:

NEW BTV SCHEDULE	
TALENT HUNT	
30 MINUTES	THE FERDY AND TRUDY SCIENCE SHOW
TOP THAT STUNT	WEDNESDAY AFTERNOON LIVE
SUGGESTION BOX	SILLIEST HOME VIDEOS
BEAR COUNTRY GLADIATORS	RIDICULOUS PET TRICKS

The new schedule was a great success.
The most popular program was *Ridiculous
Pet Tricks*. Everyone liked watching dogs
that burped and snakes that did the hula.
But it was the commercials that were the
biggest hit. They were the talk of the town.

Not that the commercials were fancy.

The one for Papa Bear's Fine Furniture just showed Papa Bear making a little speech and holding up some pieces of furniture. Farmer Ben showed so much of his fine produce that you couldn't find Farmer Ben. And Dr. Gert Grizzly just bawled everybody out for poor health habits the way she did when you went to her office.

No one was quite sure why the commer-

cials were such a hit. Maybe it was because they were so simple and corny. Maybe it was because they weren't tricky or slick like the commercials on regular television. Or maybe it was because folks got such a kick out of seeing their friends and neighbors on television.

Whatever the reason, they were a huge success. Not only did Papa, Biff Bruin, and Farmer Ben get more business, they also became overnight celebrities. As for Dr. Grizzly, her commercial didn't bring her more business. But that was only because everyone in town was already her patient.

Whether it was the corny commercials, the dog that burped, or the snake that did the hula, one thing was certain. Station BTV was the biggest thing to hit Beartown since Grizzly Gramps dug up a *T-rex* skeleton in his backyard.

Chapter 15
The Wrap Party

"What's a wrap party?" asked Brother Bear. He was walking home from school with Bonnie Brown and his usual group.

"It's a party you have in show business after you finish making a movie or putting on some kind of show," explained Bonnie. "It comes from 'wrapping things up.'"

"But all we've finished is one week of over-the-air broadcasting," said Brother.

"Yes, but what a week it was!" said Bonnie. "So I think we should cut loose and have ourselves a wrap party."

And that's just what they did. They held the party in the auditorium. The whole school was invited. There were potato chips and punch, balloons and streamers and dancing. And there were congratulations all around. But mainly for Teacher Bob. He had put the whole fabulous project together.

It was toward the end of the party that the first bombshell hit. A message came in on the principal's fax machine. Ms. Bearson, the school secretary, tore it off and brought it to Mr. Honeycomb.

When he read it, Mr. Honeycomb's party smile turned into a look of shock. He handed the fax to Teacher Bob. Though the party was nearly over, it was still pretty noisy. So not many partygoers heard the gasp that Teacher Bob let out as he read the fax.

"What's the matter, Bob?" asked Mr. Grizzmeyer, who was standing nearby. "You look like you've just been sentenced to be shot."

"Worse," said Teacher Bob. "Much worse." He handed the fax to Mr. Grizzmeyer. Then he walked slowly out of the auditorium.

Brother, Bonnie, and some of the others happened to be watching Teacher Bob and Mr. Grizzmeyer. They knew something awful had happened. But they couldn't imagine what.

Only Miss Glitch, smiling to herself in the corner, seemed to know what was going on.

Chapter 16
Comeuppance

It didn't take long for news of the fax to spread. It was from the Board of Education in Big Bear City. It had gone out to all Bear Country schools. This is what it said.

From: Board of Education
To: All Bear Country schools

To all concerned,

Five (5) days from now, all students will be tested in English, math, science, social studies, and geography. There will be no exceptions. In four (4) days, you will receive, via fax, model test sheets. These will be copied and kept under lock and key until day five (5), when the tests will be given. Testing will begin on the morning of day five (5) and will last until the closing bell.

We regret the surprise nature of these tests. But it was felt by the Board that this was the best way to measure the work of both students and teachers.

Yours truly,
Maxwell Bearhard
President, Board of Education

— — — — — — — — — — — — — — —

An emergency teachers' meeting was called for the next morning. When it started, Too-Tall was at his listening spot in the broom closet next to the faculty room. The meeting lasted a long time and ended during recess. Too-Tall heard the whole thing.

Brother, Bonnie, and the rest of the BTV crew couldn't wait to talk to Too-Tall. When they saw him coming, they knew the news was bad. Too-Tall may have been a bully.

But he was usually a happy bully. No one had ever seen him looking so unhappy before.

"Here's the story," he said with a sigh. "Teacher Bob is in big trouble. He admitted to Mr. Honeycomb and the faculty that he got carried away with BTV and didn't keep us up on our regular studies. Then he started mumbling, so I couldn't hear exactly what he said. But the idea was that he'd planned to catch up on the regular school-work when the station was running smoothly. Or something like that."

"Then what happened?" asked Queenie.

"Mr. Honeycomb said he felt bad about the whole thing but there wasn't anything he could do. Mr. Grizzmeyer and Teacher Jane stuck up for him. But not Miss Glitch."

"What did old Glitch have to say?" asked Cousin Fred.

"Something about 'pride goeth before a fall,' " said Too-Tall. "Whatever that means."

"It's Biblical," said Ferdy. "It means—"

"Shut up, Ferdy," said Queenie. "Well? What's going to happen?"

Too-Tall shrugged. "It looks like our class is gonna flunk, and Teacher Bob is gonna get fired," he said.

The group was silent.

"Oh, yeah," added Too-Tall. "One more thing. All operations at BTV are stopped until further notice."

Gloom settled over the group like a dense fog. Bonnie turned to say something to Brother. But he was already gone. He had drifted away about a minute earlier, heading for the place he always visited when he had really big problems. The rocky place in the woods near school where he could be alone with his thoughts. His Thinking Place.

So Brother wasn't around when the second bombshell hit. A police car arrived, driven by Police Chief Bruno. The chief got out of the car and entered the schoolyard. He was carrying an official-looking piece of paper.

"Hi, Dad," said Babs. "What brings you here?"

"Police business," said the chief. Then he walked into school and headed straight for the principal's office.

HI, DAD. WHAT BRINGS YOU HERE?

SORRY HERB, I DON'T EXPLAIN 'EM I JUST DELIVER 'EM.

The official-looking paper turned out to be a summons. It ordered Mr. Herbert Honeycomb to appear before the Bear Country Communications Board. He was accused of operating an illegal television station.

Chief Bruno handed the summons to Mr. Honeycomb. The principal read it and stared at the chief. He looked completely shocked. "But I don't understand, Chief," he said. "We have a license. We got it from Professor Actual Factual."

"Sorry, Herb," said Chief Bruno. "I don't

explain 'em. I just deliver 'em. Wish I didn't have to this time. I love your station. Laughed at that burping dog till I thought I'd die."

Meanwhile, Brother was deep in the woods at his Thinking Place. His special place had never failed him. But there's always a first time. Would this be it? He thought and thought and thought. But all he got for his trouble was a big blank.

"Where have you been?" Bonnie asked when Brother returned. Recess was almost over.

"At my Thinking Place," said Brother. He sounded sad. "But it was hopeless. We're all going to flunk. Except for maybe Ferdy and Trudy. And Teacher Bob is going to get fired."

"Sure, that's what'll happen," said Bonnie angrily. "That's what'll happen if all we do about it is mope around at dopey thinking places!"

"But...," said Brother.

"But, nothing," said Bonnie. "Too-Tall over there has a plan to make everybody pass the tests and save Teacher Bob's job!"

"Got that, you dimwits?" Too-Tall was saying to the class. "You're gonna cram till your brains fall out. I'm dividin' you all into study groups with a couple of smart cubs in charge of each group. It's called team teaching. Which means that if anybody flunks, my team here is gonna put out your lights! Get it?"

"Got it," said Brother. "But then again, maybe I don't get it. Since when are you so fond of Teacher Bob? He must have suspended you a dozen times."

"You *don't* get it, do you?" said Too-Tall, poking Brother in the chest with a big finger. "I'm lookin' out for myself. Here's how I see it. Teacher Bob gets fired and then what happens? Maybe Old Blood and Guts Grizzmeyer takes over the class. How would you like that? Even worse, we could get some dopey pushover for a permanent sub. How would you like *that?* So let's get crackin'! I'm puttin' you and Bonnie in charge of the math group. Now, where's that little nerd and his nerdy girlfriend?"

Brother turned to Bonnie. "I don't know if it'll work," he said. "But it's sure worth a try. Now, about this math group…"

"Wait," said Bonnie. "You don't know

about the summons yet."

"Summons?" said Brother.

Bonnie had telephoned her aunt, Lady Grizzly, from the corner phone booth. She had gotten the whole story behind the summons.

"Here's what happened," she said. "I don't have to tell you that ratings are the most important thing in the TV business. Television stations live and die by their ratings. Well, when this week's ratings for WBBC came in, Uncle Grizzly had a shock. They were as high as ever—except for the Beartown area, *where BTV wiped him out!* He was furious, of course. So he had his lawyers complain to the communications board. And the board sent Mr. Honeycomb a summons."

"Wow!" said Brother.

"It could be serious," said Bonnie. "They

could give Mr. Honeycomb a big fine."

The bell rang, ending recess. Brother and Bonnie trudged back to class. It was still morning, and already it had been quite a day. Two bombshells had hit—within minutes of each other.

Chapter 17
There's More to Life
Than Television

A week later, the cubs in Teacher Bob's class sat nervously waiting for their test results. When Teacher Bob walked in, they tried to guess the results from the look on his face. But they couldn't tell a thing.

"For Pete's sake, teach," begged Too-Tall. "How did we do?"

"Not very well," said Teacher Bob.

The nervousness turned to deep gloom.

"But you all passed!" he cried.

The cubs leapt from their seats and shouted and danced in the aisles. When the excitement finally died down, Teacher Bob

BUT YOU ALL PASSED!

tried to thank Too-Tall for what he'd done. But Too-Tall stopped him.

"Hey, you got it all wrong, teach," he said. "I was just lookin' out for myself."

"Sure you were," said Teacher Bob.

Then something happened that no one had ever seen before. Too-Tall blushed.

Things didn't work out so well for Mr. Honeycomb. When he was questioned by the communications board, he explained everything as well as he could. He told them how the popularity of the in-school system led to the over-the-air system. He told them about the unused license gathering dust in a drawer at the Bearsonian. He pointed out that BTV was just a tiny little station that broadcast only one hour a day.

The board let Mr. Honeycomb have his say. But when he was finished, the head of the board said, "While that may be an explanation, Mr. Honeycomb, it's not an excuse. The law says that Ferdy Factual is too young to use his uncle's broadcasting license. And the law is the law. We have no choice but to give you a large fine."

And that's exactly what they did.

The next morning, the cubs gathered in the schoolyard.

"We can't let Mr. Honeycomb take the rap for something *we* did," said Brother. "He's too good a guy."

The group agreed. But what could they do?

"Hmm," said Queenie. "I may have an answer. Let me check it out."

Queenie had sold a lot of commercials—

more than enough to cover the cost of the over-the-air station. But the station was now shut down. The sponsors had paid for many more commercials than they would get. A refund was in order.

When Teacher Bob heard Queenie's plan, he was glad to excuse her from class for the morning. She went straight to the sponsors and told them about the fix Mr. Honeycomb was in. She asked them to donate the extra money to help pay the fine. Most of them agreed. But there still wasn't enough money.

"I have an idea," Bonnie told Queenie. "Let me get back to you after school."

Later that day, Bonnie reached Queenie by phone. "We're all set!" she said. "Uncle Grizzly is putting up the rest of the money!"

"Great!" said Queenie. "How'd you work that?"

"It was easy," said Bonnie. "I just explained everything to Aunt Grizzly. And she told Uncle that if he didn't come up with the money, she'd invite her mother, the duchess, to come stay for a month."

Bonnie called Brother, who called Teacher Bob, who called Mr. Honeycomb, who said, "Phew!"

Of course, station BTV was taken away from Teacher Bob and the class. It would go back to being an in-school station. And a different teacher would run it each month.

Brother and Bonnie were a little sad about these changes. But only a little. Their

experience with BTV had taught them a couple of important lessons. The first was that there can be too much of a good thing. The second was that there's more to life than television.

In the meantime, Squire Grizzly kept his promise to reward the talent-hunt winner with an appearance on WBBC, the big-time station in Big Bear City. And who was the winner? Too-Tall and his rap gang!

Their appearance was a big success—so big that they got a call from a music agent. He wanted them to make a demo record in Bearville, the music capital of Bear Country.

But the agent turned out to be that well-known swindler, Ralph Ripoff. And not even Too-Tall was dumb enough to make a business deal with Ralph.

Stan and Jan Berenstain began writing and illustrating books for children in the early 1960s, when their two young sons were beginning to read. That marked the start of the best-selling Berenstain Bears series. Now, with more than one hundred books in print, videos, television shows, and even Berenstain Bears attractions at major amusement parks, it's hard to tell where the Bears end and the Berenstains begin!

Stan and Jan make their home in Bucks County, Pennsylvania, near their sons—Leo, a writer, and Michael, an illustrator—who are helping them with Big Chapter Books stories and pictures. They plan on writing and illustrating many more books for children, especially for their four grandchildren, who keep them well in touch with the kids of today.